INNER REALMS TAROT

SALEIRE

4880 Lower Valley Road • Atglen, PA 19310

Copyright © 2013 by Saleire
Library of Congress
Control Number: 2012954135

All rights reserved. No part of this work may be reproduced or used in any form or by any means—graphic, electronic, or mechanical, including photocopying or information storage and retrieval systems—without written permission from the publisher.

The scanning, uploading and distribution of this book or any part thereof via the Internet or via any other means without the permission of the publisher is illegal and punishable by law. Please purchase only authorized editions and do not participate in or encourage the electronic piracy of copyrighted materials.

"Schiffer," "Schiffer Publishing, Ltd. & Design," and the "Design of pen and inkwell" are registered trademarks of Schiffer Publishing, Ltd.

Designed by Justin Watkinson
Type set in Bookman Old Style/NewBskvll BT

ISBN: 978-0-7643-4391-9
Printed in China

Schiffer Books are available at special discounts for bulk purchases for sales promotions or premiums. Special editions, including personalized covers, corporate imprints, and excerpts can be created in large quantities for special needs. For more information contact the publisher:

Published by Schiffer Publishing, Ltd.
4880 Lower Valley Road
Atglen, PA 19310
Phone: (610) 593-1777;
Fax: (610) 593-2002
E-mail: Info@schifferbooks.com

For the largest selection of fine reference books on this and related subjects, please visit our website at
www.schifferbooks.com
We are always looking for people to write books on new and related subjects. If you have an idea for a book, please contact us at proposals@schifferbooks.com

This book may be purchased from the publisher.
Please try your bookstore first.
You may write for a free catalog.

In Europe, Schiffer books are distributed by
Bushwood Books
6 Marksbury Ave.
Kew Gardens
Surrey TW9 4JF England
Phone: 44 (0) 20 8392 8585;
Fax: 44 (0) 20 8392 9876
E-mail: info@bushwoodbooks.co.uk
Website: www.bushwoodbooks.co.uk

Dedication

Thank you,
Sparrow Hawk,
for teaching me
to trust in Spirit.

Acknowledgments

My dear Ma, whose knowledge always fascinated me.
My husband, Arie, for his patience and support
  when I needed a hand to hold.
My son, Joe, whose unconditional love
  guides me ever upward.
Pete Schiffer and his wonderful publishing company,
  whose presentation of my work has left me
  speechless and so proud.
Dinah Roseberry, whose patience and skills are amazing.

Thank you!

Contents

Introduction: Let Your Spirit Guide You

5

CHAPTER 1: **You Are the Boss**

8

CHAPTER 2: **Three Famous Spreads**

13

CHAPTER 3: **The Major and Minor Cards**

19

CHAPTER 4: **Other Meanings**

124

Conclusion

128

About the Authour

128

Introduction
Let Your Spirit Guide You

I have tried to create cards that are a quick and easy reference to the basic idea of Tarot. You do not have to spend years learning the symbolism of Tarot before you can become a wonderfully caring Tarot reader. All you have to do is trust your inner guide, your senses, feelings, emotions, and thoughts. This is something books cannot teach you. A reader wants to help people: This is the key and the only qualification you need to become the best.

The artworks are deliberately dreamy and soft, of a world where Cups are made of blue light and Swords are made of swirling energy to set your imagination free—a world of dreams and magical things where you can let go of the mundane and invite your senses to reach out to the world of inspiration and intuition. Meditation with the images is important, as this will give you the insight into what the cards mean to you. The words on the cards show you where the reading is going, but it will only be when you can let go of the constant chatter in your head that you will be able to help the Querent.

I invite you to learn the Tarot of the spiritual world, a place where guidance is readily available and freely given. If you to reach into this world, by letting go of ego and control and handing over the reading to your main spirit guide or guardian, you will create a reading that will inspire and encourage those who ask for guidance.

The Tarot is not fortune telling; nor is it a means to tell people how to live their lives; it is a way to help them *live* their lives to the fullest, through your intuitive vision and the cards' guidance. You can become a beam of light in the darkness of indecision or uncertainty. You can help people move forward, with hope and strength in their hearts, by letting the cards speak to you and share their secrets. Look at them as you would a good friend who *always* tells you the truth. Trust in their guidance, no matter how unlikely it seems at first; only time will tell if they are correct. So trust for now, and let them do their magic by helping them to reach into the corners of your mind that allow you to see beyond the ordinary.

Let the colors and the fluidity of the artwork soothe and calm you. Let it wash over you and fill you with beautiful images that sail through your thoughts, adding new dimensions to your readings. Let your spirit guide you forward in your quest to become a compassionate, loving, and healing reader. For that is what you can do with your cards: Receive guidance for yourself and heal people, by showing them a way to move forward in all areas of their lives. You can set them free from a worry and give them insight into their problems; remember this and reach out to them with your cards, your heart, and your spirit.

Chapter 1
You Are the Boss

When I bought my first deck of Tarot cards, I treated them like gold dust. I was afraid to shuffle them in case they wore out too quickly. I could not wait to begin my first reading, but when I read the book, my head spun! There was just too much information to take in—too many spreads, pairings, and extra knowledge that I did not need to know until later. The sheer volume of information overwhelmed me. I thought I was never going to learn it all and felt terribly dismayed.

I do not want that to happen to you. I want you to take your time, enjoy your cards, and let them speak to you. I want you to read the cards and *not* let them dictate to you. They are only a guide, but you are the interpreter of that guidance received through your senses and intuition. *Feel* what they are saying to you, rather than rely on just the provided meanings.

You are the boss! Whatever your instincts are telling you about the cards, believe them, because they are the right interpretations.

The truth and the wonder of a perfect reading comes from you, not from the cards. They just guide you through the life of the Querent and show you the prospects and challenges awaiting them.

When you shuffle your deck, take note of what you feel. What are you sensing about your deck? What are the emotions surrounding them? Do not worry if you do not feel anything yet; you will in time. The first thing to remember is to jot down anything that pops into your head. Trust your instincts, allow yourself to make mistakes, and take your time to become familiar with your deck. Practice with the cards and write your feelings down. Your first impressions of a card, when you are doing a reading, is probably the correct one; trust it.

Practice until you get used to holding your cards and know the spreads, so you do not have to keep remembering where the cards go. Try an easy spread first and keep to that until it feels right to move on to another one. The reason you do this is to stay focused on your feelings and not the position of the cards. If you are focusing on where the cards should be in relation to the spread, you are using your mind instead of your senses.

When you open the deck, imagine them surrounded in light and let that light flow into your heart. Let the cards become one with you, their energy fill your heart with the knowing that they will not let you down. Trust in them and let them guide you forward in your knowledge of the Tarot. In doing this, you let your guides in the world of spirit know that you want to use this tool as a means to help others and they will respect that. You will receive far more that way, than if you read a million books on the subject.

I tell you this because each person who looks at the cards will *see* the same thing, but interpret it differently. Therefore, the image itself is not the key. Both will see Pentacles, but one will think of gold and another will think of security. Both are right, but if you *sense* what the card means, you will interpret it far more efficiently. When you look at the card, you will see the gold and the meaning of security, but you may also sense that it relates to the Querent's father or his job and therefore you will have a better understanding of this card in relation to the whole reading for that particular person.

The cards show a map of a person's life and you are the interpreter of that map. You can see the cards representing people, struggles, and so on, but if you seek to know deeper meanings, sense your way around the map and feel what they are showing you, then the Querent will have a better understanding of how his or her life is shaping up.

While doing a reading, ask the Querent to relax; and take your time, don't rush it—let yourself daydream over the cards, feel them. Close your eyes and ask for guidance and then, and only then, speak. You will see images, feel emotions, a fear maybe, or a sense of loss; but remember, these emotions and feelings are to do with the Querent's life and do not belong to you, unless, of course, you are reading for yourself.

When a reading is over, rub your hands together, and release the energy of the last Querent's reading before you begin the next reading, as energy can linger. Remember, everything you feel, think, or sense during a reading has to do with the Querent. If you feel something physical, like a headache, remember, it belongs to them and not to you. These feelings are only to help you understand what is happening in the Querent's life, so be aware of this, and remember to let it go afterwards.

Okay, it is time to open your deck and begin the process of saying hello to your cards. They will become old friends; some you will be glad to see when they pop up in a reading and there will be some that you will dread. I used to read for a friend of mine and the Nine of Wands kept showing up, advising that she must be patient. I begged the cards to find another way; but no, it kept popping up because that was what she needed to hear. My sister hated the moving card, the Four of Wands, and each time it showed up in the reading, I wanted to run out the door. The cards just tell you the truth and it is up to you to believe in them and not worry about the answers.

One last word on readings: If you see something negative, don't pass it on, only pass on love and light through the cards. In that sense, I mean if you feel there is a loss coming up, prepare them, guide them, but do not blurt out: *Oh, my God, you are losing your house!* I know you would not do this, but you would be surprised how many people would be that direct.

Are you ready? Step into the wonderful, mysterious world of the Tarot and let your heart speak to you and your love fill the cards. Take your first steps to becoming the best intuitive reader you can be, by using your heart, your senses, your guide's wisdom, and your own individual interpretation of the cards to help others.

Chapter 2
Three Famous Spreads

In this chapter, I will show you the layout of three spreads, keeping them simple, so you can get started on your readings. Remember, you can change the words on the cards if you like. For instance, you could consider:

- What happened

- How the incident affects the present situation

- What can the Querent do about it

You can ask the cards whatever comes to mind to find the best solution to the problem.

The Three-Card Spread

The three-card spread is handy for finding a quick diagnosis of a problem.

Card 1: Past
The **past** always influences the present, so remember to link the cards when reading.

Card 2: Present
The **present** tells how the situation looks now.

Card 3: Future
The **future** tells the possible outcome.

The Horseshoe Spread

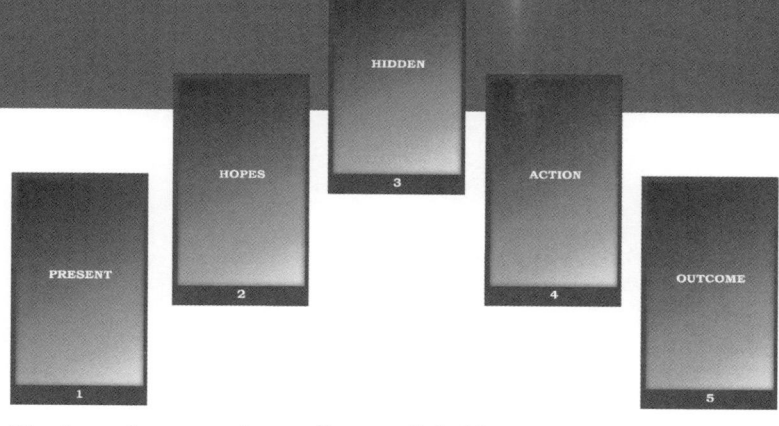

The horseshoe spread can tell you a little bit more about the Querent's situation and is easy to remember.

Card 1: Present
　　Influences around the Querent.

Card 2: Hopes
　　Hopes for the future.

Card 3: Hidden
　　The **hidden** influences are important; this might be something the querent is overlooking and therefore could be a barrier to a successful outcome, if not addressed.

Card 4: Action

If you notice, something here that needs working on, the **action** card is the way to go about changing the situation for the better.

Card 5: Outcome

If the first cards are adhered to, the **final outcome** will tell you how the path could turn out, but as in all readings, the action taken, the knowledge gained about the situation, and realistic hopes of the Querent are what make the final outcome successful. In the end, it all comes down to free will.

The Celtic Cross Spread

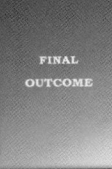

The Celtic-cross spread can tell you a lot more about the Querent's situation.

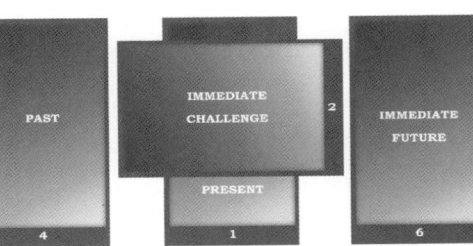

Card 1: Present
   What is **ongoing** in the Querent's life.

Card 2: Immediate Challenge
   Immediate **obstacle** to overcome.

Card 3: Source
   The **source** tells you what is causing the problem.

Card 4: Past
Where the problem began.

Card 5: Expectations
The **expectations** of the Querent tells you what they hope will happen.

Card 6: Immediate Future
The not-too-distant future.

Card 7: You
The **you** card in this spread is important; it shows you how the Querent is feeling about themselves. You can tell a lot from this and how the situation is often influenced by how we see ourselves; look to the next card to see if this is realistic or not.

Card 8: How Others See You
How the Querent presents him/herself to the world.

Card 9: Truth of the Matter
The **truth of the matter** leaves the bare bones of the situation for you to examine.

Card 10: Final Outcome
What **result** the Querent can expect.

Do they all match up, or is there something niggling at you after reading the cards? If so, try putting three more cards around the card that is worrying you. That way you can be sure if you've got it right or not, and will also see what is influencing that card.

Chapter 3
The Major and Minor Cards

Here you will find the meanings of the cards. I have not included the meanings of reversed cards, as I feel the upright say all that is needed to say. I have also added space for you to record your first impressions. This will help you to make your cards more personal. Do not worry if your ideas do not match up with those shown; first impressions are unique to you. Build a solid foundation for future readings by meditating on each card and then filling in these parts of the book with as much information as you can, recording thoughts, feelings, sensations, and colors. If it feels right, jot it down. This is your store of goodies to dip into when you need inspiration. Let us see what we come up with together.

The Major Arcana herald a major event, the main event, and the Minor Arcana provide the influences around that event in the Querent's life. The major cards show the journey through life, and the minor just add to the experience by revealing the people, feelings, emotions, and happenings associated with the Querent.

MAJOR

ARCANA

0 | The Fool

You are off on a journey with no clue where it will take you, but you must trust in your instincts, be brave, and move forward. You feel carefree and full of the joys of spring. Nothing is going to stop you on this journey; you are ready to take on the world and enjoying every minute of it. Trust that this new path is the one for you; it will take you to new adventures that you will revel in like a child. Be open, but watch out for those first few steps into wonderland—they could be a bit precarious and full of unexpected hitches. This card tells you that if you trust in yourself you will go a long way. Be prepared for the journey of a lifetime.

FIRST IMPRESSIONS

I THE MAGICIAN

Resources　　　Awareness

Action　　　　Power

I | Magician

You are on your way and have a goal in mind. Do not let anything take your focus away for a moment; you have the ability to see this through. It is time to go all out to fulfill your dreams and make them a reality. You have the power and the expertise to do this; believe in your creativity, and send it out to the universe with all the energy you can muster. You must act now and believe in miracles; there is one on the way, as long as you are sure of what you want. Imagine a footballer heading for a goal, but unsure which side he is on. You have the power, but you must know which goal you are heading for and why. Move forward with confidence and concentrate on the target. You have all you need to win.

FIRST IMPRESSIONS

II HIGH PRIESTESS

Psychic

Influential

Secretive

Knowing

Oracle

II | High Priestess

Seek within yourself for the answers, paying attention to your instincts, rather than trying to use reason. The answer to a question lies deep within you, so you must meditate—find a quiet place to contemplate and you will find the truth. There is something happening in your life where you will need to use your intuition, so trust your inner voice. Look beyond the obvious explanation in this situation and dig deeper; there is something hidden that you must uncover. You have psychic ability and can often tell when the phone is going to ring or someone is going to call. Use this ability to find out what is going on around you and trust in the answers you get back.

FIRST IMPRESSIONS

III EMPRESS

Promise

Femininity

Creativity

Assurance

III | Empress

Everything to do with home, children, and nurturing influences surrounds you. There is an abundance of love and laughter. You attract this because you act with tenderness and compassion in all situations. You are a born healer, nurturing everyone you meet and taking care of his or her needs. You love all that Mother Earth provides and are happiest in the countryside, picking daisies, and having a picnic with family and friends. You enjoy your home and feel rich and full of joy because you understand the real meaning of happiness. Your family means everything to you and you do all in your power to make them feel loved.

FIRST IMPRESSIONS

IV THE EMPEROR

Protection
Commanding
Leadership

Growth
Strength
Regulation

IV | The Emperor

Father figure, authoritative and in control, this man is the head of the household and keeps order where there is chaos. He is the regulator, the boss, a leader, and a guide. He stands for no nonsense, gives good advice, and is the epitome of tradition. He abides by the law, sticks to the rules, and adds a few more regulations just for good measure. He keeps things steady and protects his family with all his might. He is a force to behold and a good role model. The Emperor cherishes family life and is a good provider. He does not shirk his duties; he takes pride in them and wants nothing more than to provide a safe, secure, and orderly home for his family. This man will help you find order out of chaos.

FIRST IMPRESSIONS

V | Hierophant

This card states that you are traditional in what you believe in and follow the rules and regulations put down by others. You like to fit in and be part of the crowd. It is time to find out more about something; it may be that you have questions about your faith or just your life in general and you need answers. It is up to you to study—seek out the knowledge that will help you expand in all areas of your life and your beliefs. You may be stuck in traditional patterns and feel restricted by the laws of old. It is time to move forward through knowledge and a knowing that the universe is calling you to expand, open up to new possibilities and a new way of thinking.

MAJOR ARCANA

FIRST IMPRESSIONS

VI | The Lovers

It is time for love! Watch out, here it comes! This card signals a new lover, relationship, or marriage. There is a lovely sense of security with this love, a safe feeling, a knowing that you are home. If you are not open to love, then start thinking about this and make the change, because it is out there for you. All you need to do is open the door.

The Lovers card is all about getting closer, building the bonds, and cherishing the people you love. Have a lovely romantic evening; go that extra mile to show you care and you will be glad you did. If you are tempted to new pastures, try to think of the love you have now and ask yourself: Is it worth it, or do I have all the love I need right here and now?

FIRST IMPRESSIONS

VII | The Chariot

You have a task to perform, a new path to choose from, or a job to complete, and this will take all your concentration and willpower to finish. Try to focus all this power into making the right decision and do not let anyone distract you from your goal. You will have success if you are doggedly determined to win. You **can** win and you will win; **know** this. Use all your powers of self-control, confidence, and concentration to achieve this goal; it will be worth it when you stand victorious. You will beat the competition, if you believe in yourself and your ability to control your emotions and use your will to grab that prize.

FIRST IMPRESSIONS

VIII STRENGTH

Courage

Balance

Patience

Strength

Compassion

VIII | Strength

You have the inner strength to guide you through this situation. When people are goading you into losing control, making you lose your temper, you will rise to the occasion with a calmness that will shock everyone. You know that true strength is not brute force. It takes a very powerful being to use self-control in a situation that would send everyone else over the edge. You have this power and can put it to good use. Be calm, serene, and gentle in reaching out and silencing the opposition. You are in control of the situation and that is all you need to know. Try compassion, love, and tenderness when you feel the need to explode and you will win the day.

FIRST IMPRESSIONS

IX THE HERMIT

Wisdom Solitude Humility

Seeking Detachment

IX | The Hermit

It is time to seek within for answers, realize your path, and know that you are going in the right direction. You need this time to put things in perspective, contemplate, and relax. You are reading, studying, and searching everywhere for the answers, but sometimes the only thing you need to do is ask yourself one question: Am I happy? If the answer is no, then you have work to do by seeking the truth about your life and **why** you are not happy. Look deeper into the meaning of life, and know where you stand. Ask again: Am I happy? If not, change your life and progress further along the path of truth.

FIRST IMPRESSIONS

X | Wheel of Fortune

Luck is with you! It is a time of miracles manifesting in your life, so take a chance and realize your dream. They might manifest through gold, a win on the lottery perhaps, or through that job you have always wanted—and it may even involve love. Therefore, be alert, watch for opportunities that only come once in a lifetime. Be ready to rejoice in the miracle of miraculous manifestations that could change your life. Now is the time to keep your eyes and ears open and believe in your instincts; they will lead you to greater things and fulfill your dreams. It is time to wake up to miracles.

MAJOR ARCANA

FIRST IMPRESSIONS

XI | Justice

You are trying to do the right thing by being fair and treating everyone equally. This is a good thing and is the only way you are going to solve the situation that has arisen. Try to use all your powers of reasoning and judge accordingly. Weigh all the sides before you make the decision. Is there something you are being too emotional about and need to cool down before you take action?

Take your time, be fair to all concerned, view it from all sides, and then (and only then) make your decision. Make it your business to find out all the pros and cons before you judge the situation or move ahead. It will give you peace in the end because you will have made the right decision, based on fact, not fiction.

FIRST IMPRESSIONS

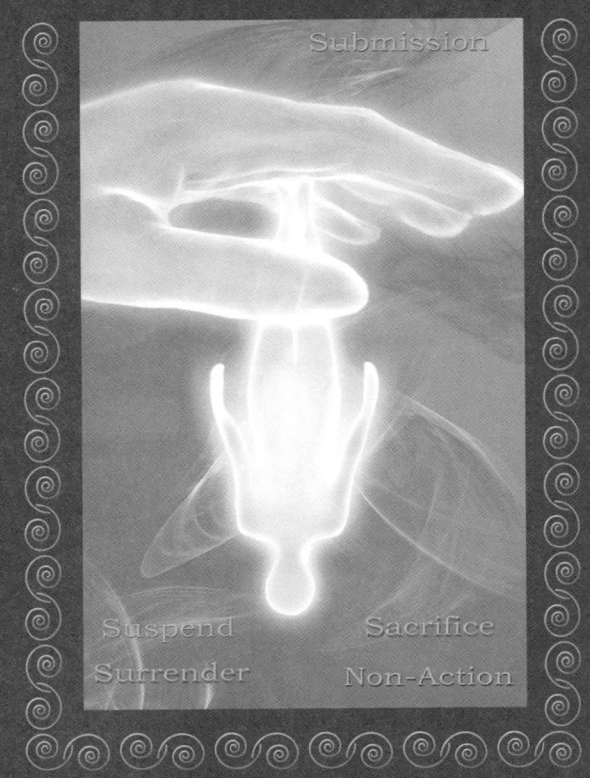

XII | The Hanged Man

This is a time for reflection and meditation. Sometimes no action is the best action. Wait, hold back, and ponder the situation at hand. It may be that you need spiritual inspiration to help you understand or gain insight into how to move forward.

You may feel that you have been blocked or left behind, but this is not the case. The universe is in control now, so take a leap of faith and let things happen of their own accord. You have no control in this matter, so give up the fight and let the spirit guide you.

Things will change in time, and you will see that the holding back was necessary and right. Trust and believe that the situation is in hand, just not **your** hands for now.

FIRST IMPRESSIONS

XIII DEATH

Change

Action

Exposure

Termination

XIII | Death

Ring out the old and ring in the new. This card is the card of endings and new beginnings. A relationship might have run its course, a job fails to live up to expectations, or your car has seen better days and needs renewing. It is not a sign of doom and gloom, though you might think it at the time; it is a time of rejoicing. Spring is on its way into your life and the old wintery cold is on its way out.

Mourn the old; let it go in peace and give thanks that you have learned from this experience, but relish the thought that now you can move into a new and more exciting phase of your life. Watch for new beginnings. This card demands a spring-cleaning of your life, to make way for something better able to move you forward on your life's journey.

FIRST IMPRESSIONS

XIV TEMPERANCE

Healing

Merging

Chemistry

Fluidity

XIV | Temperance

Sometimes a situation comes along which asks us to look deep within for solutions. This is one of those times where you will need to use all of your abilities to find balance. Brew a potion, make a cup of tea, suggest a sauna, or go for a swim—whatever it takes to bring balance and harmony within you or the people you are helping.

Most times it only takes a soothing chat to keep things on par; other times it might need a strong shoulder to bear the burden. Either way, a situation that needs calming and a mix of skills to sort it out is coming. Meet this challenge by searching deep within and you will find that you have something to bring to the table, as mediator or mentor, which will help move this along.

FIRST IMPRESSIONS

XV THE DEVIL

Compulsion

Loss

Addiction

Ego

XV | The Devil

Say hello to The Devil in your life. What is it, or who is it that you are obsessing over and are blind to? Often when we are too absorbed in a situation, we cannot see the way forward—we are in the dark, so to speak—but this does not have to be permanent. Shine a light on the situation and see where there is need for improvement. A good clearing out should reveal where the creepy crawlies are hiding. When you find them, banish them from your life and let the obsession disappear in the hope of a new day. There is nothing stopping you from having a better life, other than your inability to let things go. If they are not making you feel good, then you can step aside and move along.

FIRST IMPRESSIONS

XVI THE TOWER

Revelation

Awakening

Realisation

Sudden Change

XVI | The Tower

The Tower imagery frightens the living daylights out of people because it shows that chaos is about to happen. But wait, this might be necessary for you to see a new opportunity to progress. Changes—big changes, surprising changes, and changes that make you sit up and notice—are on the way. Do not worry, they are not always bad. If you think about it, when was the last time you really looked at your life to see where you were heading? When was the last time you did something exciting, fresh, and creative?

It is time for the universe to take a hand in your life to show you something that needs changing quickly. If you do not make it happen, the universe will, so let go of the old and look forward to a surprising new beginning. It might not seem that great at first, but change is always good, so try not to kick and scream too much, because when you look back, you will be thankful this happened.

FIRST IMPRESSIONS

XVII | The Star

A star appearing in your reading is a lovely thing to see. It brings hope and inspiration. You will see things more clearly now, while that beautiful star is shining down on the situation. You have wished, hoped, and made this happen by sending out all that beautiful energy into the universe. Now it has come back to you, *tenfold*. Remember to share the joy you are feeling with others, as this is a spiritual and loving time and one you will look back on with contentment.

A star is a guide, so watch out for inspiration in the most unlikely of places—in the clouds, for instance, or at the bus stop. Every word you hear, every sight you see, and every feeling you have could hold a message for you. Let your spirit show you how beautiful its song is when you listen with an open heart.

FIRST IMPRESSIONS

XVIII | The Moon

Ah, the moon. It shines a delicate light on our world of darkness and inspires us to create and dream of romance while under its magical influence. It reflects back to us the fantasy of our dreams, dreams that may not be so realistic and can often be misleading. Maybe you have let the moon affect your emotions and you are unsure of how to deal with a situation that has arisen. Do not worry; let this phase pass quietly into the sunshine of day and you will see clearly again.

FIRST IMPRESSIONS

XIX THE SUN

Joy

Assurance

Enthusiasm

Vitality

Expansion

XIX | The Sun

The sun is shining in our lives and is glowing all around us. This is a wonderful time; it shows great vitality, warmth, and nourishment is here, or on its way. This is a time for putting your feet up and relaxing with family. Take a holiday; you deserve it. Have a barbecue and invite family and friends. This is a time for sharing the gifts of the earth. We feel nurtured, loved, and content with this card. Happy days are here to stay. The Sun can shine on all your problems and make them seem like nothing, so whatever cards are near this one, do not worry if they are a bit disconcerting. The Sun will lessen the blow.

FIRST IMPRESSIONS

XX | Judgement

Judgement is a wonderful card of enlightenment. If you have chosen this card, then it means you are about to discover something about yourself that puts you on the right path. You may find your true mission in life, attend a service at church and feel embraced by the light, or you might just wake up and feel that you know what you really want. You have a discerning eye at this time, and can see what is right and wrong in your life. Use this time to make the right choices because you are in a position to do so now. Let love shine into your heart when making these choices and you will not go wrong.

FIRST IMPRESSIONS

XXI | The World

The World is here to show you that you have made it! Thank God! It was a journey and a half to get here, but you have, and you can rest at ease because everything is looking rosy and you are full of the joys of spring. Whatever you attempt now has a very good chance of succeeding, so go for it with all the gusto you can muster. Life is your playground now: laugh, rejoice. Be happy, jump up and down; you are a success!

FIRST IMPRESSIONS

MINOR

ARCANA

King of Pentacles

This person has made it. He may be a banker, an entrepreneur, an accountant, or just a wealthy man. The coins, carefully positioned, mean he has thought about this, put in the work, and accumulated a fortune. The wings of gold say he is secure, safe in his knowledge of finances—this man knows how to make money.

If you are looking for advice about your finances, this is a good card. Generous with his wealth, the King of Pentacles often sponsors a good cause. He will gladly review your proposal. He works hard and is reliable. You can trust this man. He has skills and uses them wisely. He likes to share his knowledge, so is a good friend, a generous boss, or a wise financial advisor.

FIRST IMPRESSIONS

Queen of Pentacles

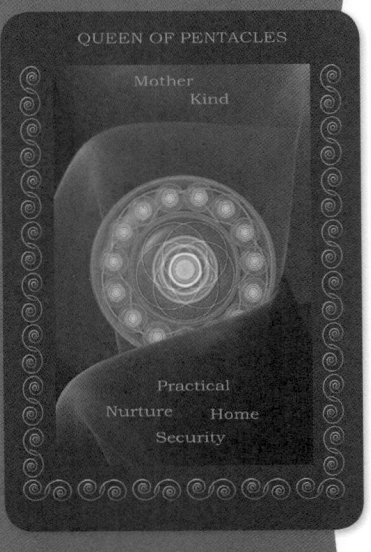

This woman could make a dinner out of the rind of a slice of bacon, watch over ten children, do the gardening, and still have time to play with the dog. She is versatile, practical, home-loving, and gentle in her approach.

She would give you the coat off her back, generous to a fault. She is a good mother, a gentle lover, and gives everything in abundance. You will not want for anything if this woman is in your life. She is maternal and mothers everyone around her. She is loving and supportive, healing you with her gentle nature. You will find this woman in a caring environment: a mother, nurse, healer, therapist, or doctor. She excels in these areas.

FIRST IMPRESSIONS

Knight of Pentacles

This man is younger than the king, but is meticulous in his attempts, maybe too fussy in his pursuit of perfection. He has a tendency to work too hard, pay too much attention to detail, and forget to enjoy the journey. He is hard working and likes nothing better than to add up the accounts and keep everything running smoothly. He is unwavering, full of energy, and wants to succeed. The feeling with him is that he is a young manager, trying to make his way to the top, willing to work all hours, hoping for riches, but not without putting the work in. This is the man you want working for you; he is thorough in all he does.

KNIGHT OF PENTACLES

Cautious
Thorough
Realistic
Unwavering

FIRST IMPRESSIONS

Conclusion

Now it is time to leave you and let you find your way around the cards. Remember to trust your instincts and enjoy your journey into Tarot. It should not be a complicated path, and you do not have to remember the meanings of each card. All you have to do is trust your instincts and your intuition. Believe in your own interpretations. If you do all your readings out of love and compassion, wanting to help your Querent find their way, then you will become a wonderfully gifted Reader.

It only remains for me to thank you for choosing *Inner Realms Tarot* and leave you with this little bit of advice: Let the Spirit move you, the cards guide you, and your heart deliver the message.

About the Author

Saleire is a qualified, Spiritualists' National Union (SNU) healer, author, inspirational artist, and spiritual medium, but her true mission in life is to be a qualified human being.

Pairings of Court Cards

King and King	Strong influences around external affairs
Queen and Queen	Two very strong women influencing you
Knight and Knight	Adults or teens who have opposing ideas
Page and Page	Two young people who you care about

Pairings of Aces

Cups and Swords	Love and honesty in relationship
Cups and Pentacles	Secure in your love
Cups and Wands	Emotional, creative energy
Wands and Pentacles	Excitement and abundance
Wands and Swords	Courage and intelligence
Swords and Pentacles	Intelligence and prosperity

Pairings of Suits

Cups and Cups	Emotional time
Cups and Swords	Trust your heart
Cups and Wands	Spiritual time
Cups and Pentacles	Take action
Wands and Wands	Passionate times
Wands and Pentacles	Go for it
Wands and Swords	Inspirational
Swords and Swords	Philosophical
Swords and Pentacles	Whirlwind
Pentacles and Pentacles	Steady

Chapter 4
Other Meanings

The cards influence each other, just as people do when they are together. I will show you some of the pairings here to give a wider scope into your cards and their meanings. When you are ready, you will do more seeking and find more knowledge; for now, just relax and know that the universe will carry you forward in your studies when it is right for you to do so.

Here are some basic meanings to begin with:

Zodiac Signs

Cups	Water	Pisces	Cancer	Scorpio	Feelings
Wands	Fire	Aries	Leo	Sagittarius	Energy
Swords	Air	Aquarius	Gemini	Libra	Thought
Pentacles	Earth	Taurus	Virgo	Capricorn	Action

Ace of Swords

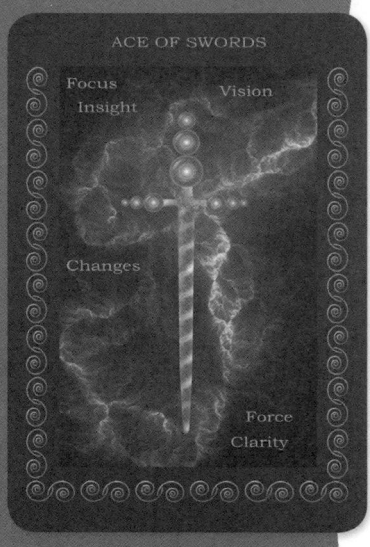

If you want to find out the truth in a situation, this is the card to do it. You will have all you need to make the right choice. Gather all the information available to you and cut through to the crux of the matter. See what is real, not illusion, and make that choice. It might be that you want to cut someone out of your life, but you are letting emotion surround this decision in a fog. Cut through this fog and see them as they really are, and then make your choice. If it is a new job, do you really want to work all the hours God sends, or could you find a better one, more appropriate to your needs? See what other cards are around this one and know that a decision has to be made soon.

FIRST IMPRESSIONS

2 Swords

Do not sit on the fence when it comes to making a decision or you will miss experiencing something wonderful. It is time to make that all-important choice and take the plunge. What do you have to lose? You are a thinker and can make good choices, so believe in this, work out all the angles, and move forward. It may be two jobs. Analyze them, see ahead, and go for the one that will bring you the most happiness. If it is two lovers, that is easy; who makes you laugh, feel nurtured and makes you want to spend every moment with them? If it is two problems, separate them and see them from afar; let emotions go, and think about the options that you have open to you.

FIRST IMPRESSIONS

3 Swords

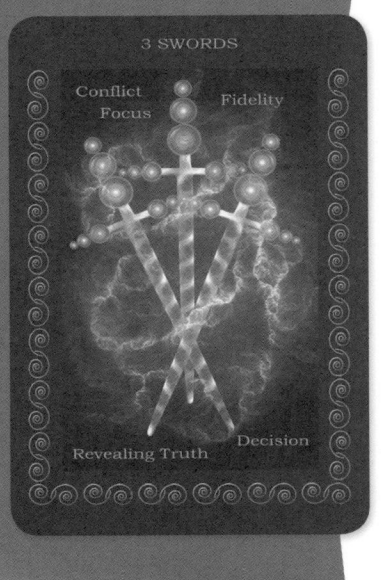

You feel betrayed, let down, and hurt by someone else. You may even feel sick to your stomach that someone could be so callous. Sometimes, all you need in this situation is to let go, forgive and move on—what else can you do? If you hang on to the pain, you will become miserable and unable to carry on with your life. So let it go; it is not worth the anguish. Think about it: Only your ego and pride was hurt. Your spirit, the *real* you, is not hurt at all and you *will* live to face another day. You will find a better way, even if it does not look like it now. Trust and believe that the changes that occurred are good for you and herald something better. Believe you deserve better and it will come faster.

FIRST IMPRESSIONS

4 Swords

It is time to have a lovely restful holiday or a relaxing massage. You can meditate, go to the beach, take time for yourself, or just go for a walk, because this is a time to listen to that inner voice and take stock of where you are going in life. Sometimes in the hustle and bustle of life, we are caught up in other people's lives and forget our dreams and wishes. So forget the chores; go outside, lie down in the grass, and pay attention to your dreams. Take some time to remember where you are going and where you want to be in the future. Make this your time to say to the universe that you are still waiting for that dream to come true!

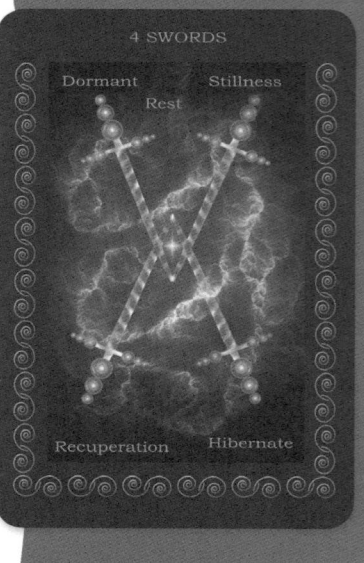

FIRST IMPRESSIONS

5 Swords

When this card appears in your reading you have to ask yourself two questions: Am I being selfish, or is someone around me taking me for granted? There is nothing wrong with taking care of your needs, as long as you remember to share with others and consider their needs, too. On the other hand, if you are self-sacrificing, then you forget to honor yourself and this is wrong. Try to find the balance. If you are in an abusive situation, put yourself first and get out of there; but if you are being selfish, apologize profusely and learn to treat others the way you would like to be treated. The conflict you experience is because you are not treating others right or vice versa. Change it by looking within for the answers.

FIRST IMPRESSIONS

6 Swords

You may need a holiday—a time to recuperate and take stock of your life. Life is a bit of a pain at times and can make you feel exhausted and depressed when it is not to your liking, but this is only a red flag telling you that it is time to change. It may be that you need to rethink the situation you are in and move on, or find a better way to deal with it, or it may be that you need to change your way of thinking about things. Take a trip, keep your head high, and analyze your situation. While you are away in calmer waters, you will find the answer to your question.

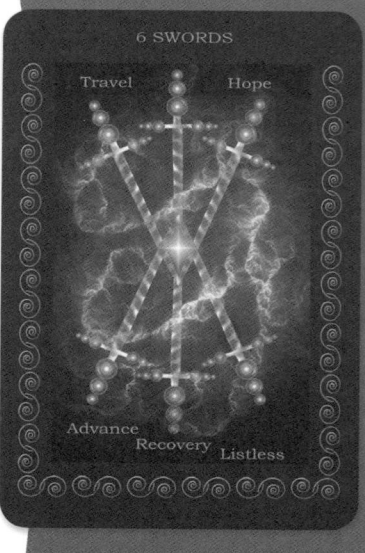

FIRST IMPRESSIONS

7 Swords

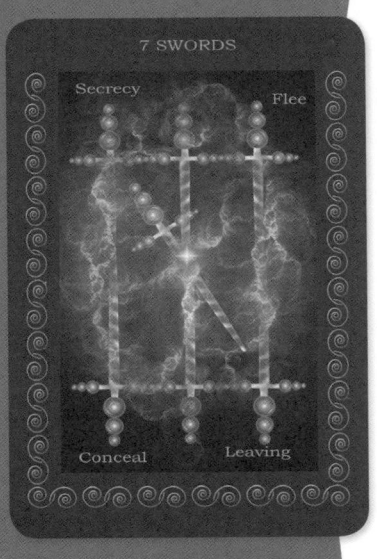

It is time to face the truth. Are you running away from a situation because you just do not know how to cope with it, or have you done something that you know is wrong and cannot face the person you hurt? Either way, it is time to admit your weakness and deal with it; hiding from it will not make you feel any better. Face it head on and know the real reason behind your fear. Fear never goes away until you conquer it. So take a deep breath, deal with the problem directly, and try not to run away. If you do not succeed, try again; you will win self-respect and the feeling that you have achieved something of importance if you chase away the inner demons of fear.

FIRST IMPRESSIONS

Do not be a victim in the present situation; stand firm. If you do not know what to do, ask for advice. You cannot see a way out because you are blinded by your emotions and confused thinking. Let someone who is impartial and unemotionally attached show you the way forward. You feel as if you are paralyzed, but really, it just takes one step forward and you are free to keep going. You feel bound and tied to a situation; but again, this is not true; you can make a change, stand up for your rights, leave or get help. There are a million choices and a million ways to go about it, but you need to make the first assertive step toward freedom.

8 Swords

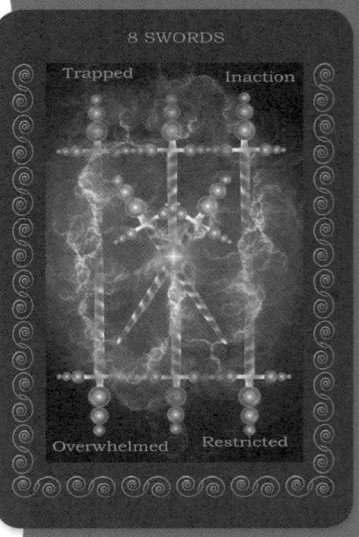

FIRST IMPRESSIONS

9 Swords

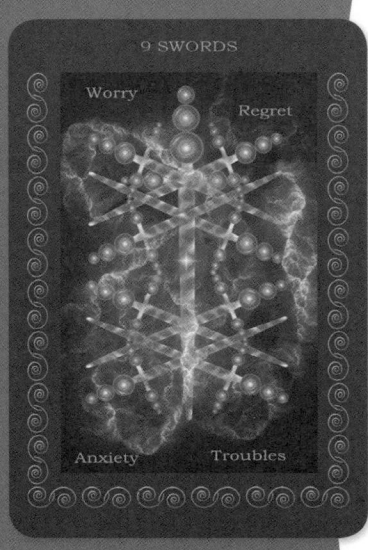

Stop doubting in your abilities; worrying is not going to make it any better. Allow this time to pass and get on with other things. It is a time when you really need to get a grip on your emotions and not allow them to rule you. Stop feeling sorry for yourself and do something about it.

Make a choice: If it is something that is hurting you, let it go; if it is something you desire, work hard for it; at least then you know you gave it your best shot. There is no gain in despair; let it go and move on to greener pastures. Do not waste another moment thinking all is lost; it is not. The only thing that might be lost is your pride. Be strong, face the day, and let the universe send you something better.

FIRST IMPRESSIONS

10 Swords

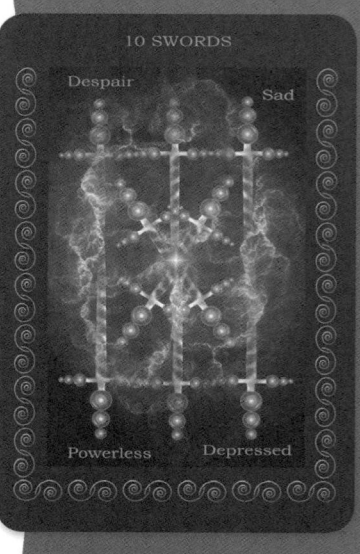

You have let yourself fall into the trap of self-depreciation and lack of self-worth. You've let others take the lead, sacrificing your goals and putting your needs at the bottom of the list. You are feeling depressed and wondering why life keeps pushing you down; but to be honest, you have allowed this to happen.

You do not love or respect yourself enough to put yourself first, so how can you expect others to do so? Gather what energy you have left and start loving and nurturing the person who is most important in your life: *you*. Give yourself a pat on the back for getting this far. Be proud, step up to the plate, and take what you need to get past this stage. You can do it; you just have to believe in you.

FIRST IMPRESSIONS

Page of Swords

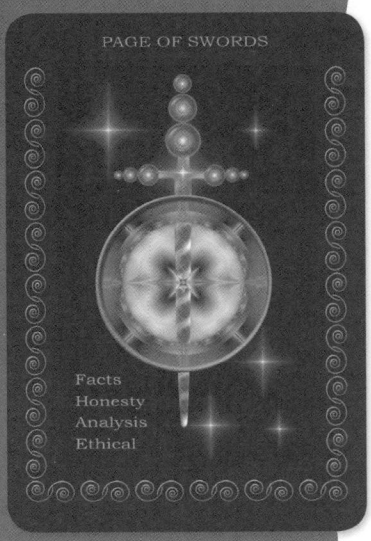

This is a time to keep your head up and use all your study skills to find out as much about the situation as you can. You must use all the powers of logic, analysis, and reason to see your way through this moment in your life. Do not let your heart rule your head; this is a time to be sharp, alert, and ready for anything. Are you being too emotional about something? Well, put your thinking cap on and see it from a different angle.

Be fair and ethical in your judgements. Now is the time to face the truth, no matter how annoying. It is time to gather your inner resolve and move forward in honesty and firm belief that you have made the right choice based on the information you have at hand.

FIRST IMPRESSIONS

Knight of Swords

The first thing you need to do when you see this card is ask, is he *for* you or *against* you? He is analytical, clear and concise, speaks plainly, tactless, and often cruel in his delivery of his opinion. If he is *for* you, then you have someone who knows his job down to the finest detail and can help you enormously in getting a project ready for promotion or sale. If he is *against* you, then you have a battle on your hands. He could be trying to hurt you with his criticism, but this will not get to you if you believe in yourself and tell him to take a walk.

He might be a bit of a know-it-all, but he is just the man you need to help you with something that needs scrutiny and honesty. So see who he is before you panic and run a mile.

FIRST IMPRESSIONS

Queen of Swords

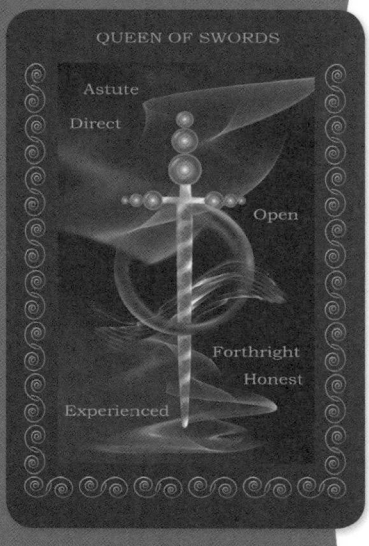

This woman plays by the rules, is upfront in all her dealings, honest in her approach, and speaks her mind. She can be a bit too blunt, but not in an awkward way. She will not embarrass you; she just tells it like it is. Getting on with things, even in the worst circumstances, is something she is easily able to do—she has been there, done that, and knows the score.

Do not try to wind this woman up or you will lose. She does not tolerate fools lightly. You will know if she likes you or not because she will tell you straight to your face. There is nothing hidden beneath the surface, nothing to mislead you; what you see is what you get. This Queen is witty, funny, and a delight to be around. Invite her to dinner and see her shine.

FIRST IMPRESSIONS

King of Swords

This man can see all sides of the situation, as he has no emotional attachment to the outcome. If you need an analytical approach, a fair answer or just someone who can give you clear, unbiased advice, this is the man to go to, as he is an excellent judge of situations and can see through the mass of confusion at an instant. He is honest in his dealings, trustworthy, and he will not take sides. If he sees that you are in the wrong, he will waste no time in telling you so, but it will be a fair judgement and one you can live with.

He does not tolerate dishonesty, so be honest with your dealings and your questions and you will do just fine with this man. Who is he? Check the cards around him to see where he comes in.

FIRST IMPRESSIONS

Ace of Wands

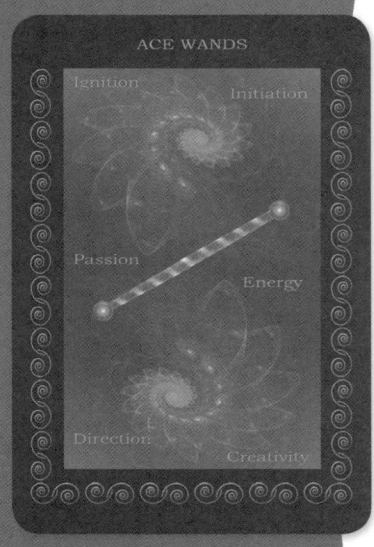

Face your fears, be assured of your abilities, and take on this fantastic challenge. It is a time to shine and expand your possibilities. You are amazing, but you need to get this fact out there. You are skilled, unique, and full of energy; now all you need do is shout out to the world that you are ready. Well, your chance is here; it is time to blow your own trumpet and proudly take the first step to a new beginning that is going to change your life.

Have faith in yourself and in your abilities and you can win whatever this card puts in front of you. See what the other cards show you to see what this is. If it is a job, then it is yours, but only if you trust in what you can do.

FIRST IMPRESSIONS

2 Wands

You are in touch with your personal power now and feel you could do anything. Time to assert yourself in the world and make them take notice of your talent and skills. If you take the initiative, you can achieve your goals. The pot of gold is there for the taking—all you have to do is take that first step.

Be a pioneer, take a risk, lead the way in whatever it is that you want to achieve, and you will win. Achievement is on the cards if you tune in to the aspects of you that make you different, unique, and a force to be reckoned with. It is this unique approach that will help you win; being **you** will bring you great success.

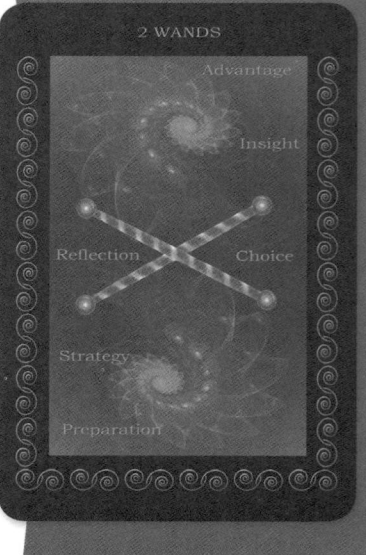

FIRST IMPRESSIONS

3 Wands

You are planning a trip, checking out new horizons, and wanting to get on your way. A new adventure is on the cards and you are ready for this. You are mulling over your options and enjoying the fact that you have secured your position in life and can now expand in all areas.

Well done; this is going to be a great time of choices and new beginnings. It might be that you are thinking about changing your job or your home. If this is the case, check out the cards that surround this one to see if it will be successful or not. Plan carefully before jumping in and you cannot go far wrong. The energy is all about moves and new horizons, so go for it; the universe is helping you progress further.

FIRST IMPRESSIONS

4 Wands

You have every right to be excited and bubble over with joy because you have earned something lovely: a new job that you love, a new house that is better than the last, or a new lover who makes you feel content. You are free to make choices and free to move on. Hit the road and sing a little tune; you are on the way to a better place and there are some lovely surprises along your new path.

This is a special time of congratulations. Celebrate with your friends and give thanks to all those who helped you. You are on an exciting new pathway and you should be jumping up and down, thrilled at the possibilities this journey opens up. You are free from all that held you down and stopped you from progressing.

FIRST IMPRESSIONS

5 Wands

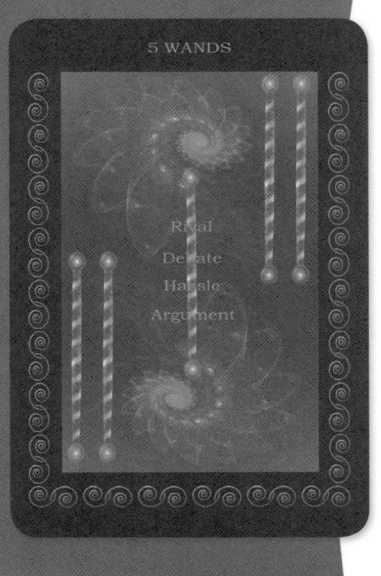

Here we go again—another day of hassles and little annoyances. But it is not going to bother you if you stand your ground and do not react to other people's quibbles and arguments. Stand clear, observe, and let it flow over you. Be calm in this situation and you will be victorious. While all around you is in chaos, your calmness and peaceful approach will be noted, so keep your head and let them battle on—it is not your war. You may have one of two who try to engage you in their fights; say no. You are above such things and you will come out on top. This is a minor setback; do not worry—it will all be over before it has even begun. You will see that it is not worth fighting over. Stay calm.

FIRST IMPRESSIONS

6 Wands

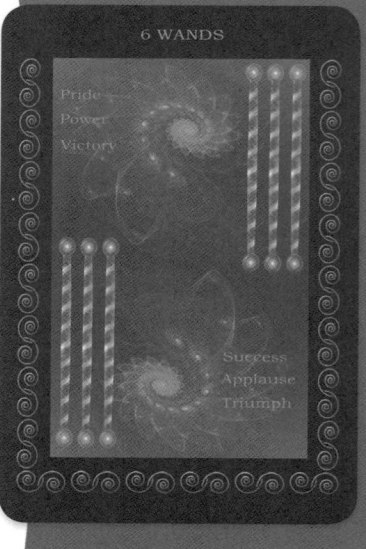

Strut your stuff; you got the job, won the battle, and reaped the rewards you so rightly earned. You are a winner! This is a card of great joy; the battle is over and you deserve that pat on the back for not giving in to despondency or allowing anyone to push you out of the picture. You are in charge of your surroundings and it feels good. You are on top of your game and victorious. Enjoy the limelight, enjoy your victory, but do not be too arrogant—remember to stay humble and thank the universe for helping you through this one. You will publicly achieve something and be a great success.

FIRST IMPRESSIONS

7 Wands

Let your voice be heard when something challenges your beliefs or your position. Be strong and defend your territory. This card signifies a time of challenge, so you need to be ready to defend relentlessly. It may be that someone is trying to usurp you out of your job; be assertive and show your strength of position by refusing to yield to their tactics. Be firm and say your piece. You have the advantage point and can see a whole lot more than the challenger, so use this information to improve your chances of winning. If applying for a job, make sure your CV/resume is in tiptop shape in order to impress your new employer and you *will* get the job.

FIRST IMPRESSIONS

8 Wands

Big news is on the way and it is practically on your doorstep. This card is all about speed; it's coming fast and you should hold your hand out now because that is how quick this new opportunity is coming. Watch for the mail or a phone call with good news. Be ready to use this information to your advantage and take the lead. You are in a strong position now. Something you are waiting for will come and the result will be victorious and to your liking. Get your skates on; this is like a lightning bolt of inspiration that gives you something to build on. Do not be slow to react on this information or else you might lose out.

FIRST IMPRESSIONS

9 Wands

Being prepared is an important position to be in, but you are being over cautious, maybe even a little paranoid? It may never happen! You have the advantage of seeing the whole picture, so make this work for you; in that sense you are more prepared than others in the scenario. You have a strong character and will protect your home and your family with gusto, but remember to relax and not let fear make you think you have to be watchful all the time. Do not close yourself off to new horizons just because you fear the outcome; have faith in your abilities and go for it.

FIRST IMPRESSIONS

10 Wands

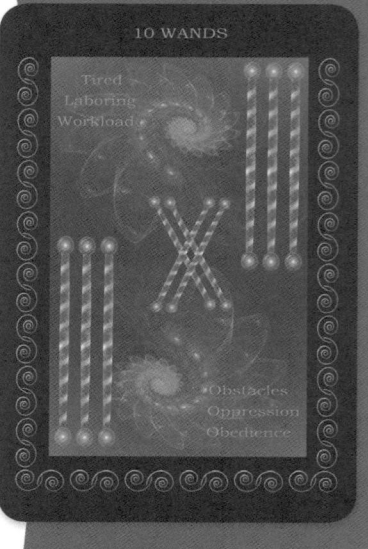

Burdens hold you down. You have taken them on yourself; no one asked you to do this, but you do not know how to let them go now. It was your choice and you are so busy with these extra hours, bills, worries, and other people's problems that you have forgotten to take time out for yourself. You could ask for help, but you are too exhausted and overcome with tiredness to contemplate this. You are afraid that if you think for a minute, you might drop the ball and chaos will pursue. But this is nonsense; take the plunge, ask for help, and see what happens. What do you have to lose, except the extra burdens?

FIRST IMPRESSIONS

Page of Wands

The Page of Wands asks you to be passionate in your approach to life. Let go of your reserves and become excited about some new venture you decide to tackle. Treat the world as your oyster; enjoy every little twist and turn in life. Be happy, joyful, and full of beans, because this energy will bring good things. A card of good news, full of promise and surprises, and something good is coming in the mail. Watch for this and know that it will be successful, if you let go of fear and believe in yourself. Be unique in your approach to the everyday challenges and do not let fear or doubt enter your head. You are a leader, if you so choose.

FIRST IMPRESSIONS

Knight of Wands

This card heralds a journey that requires great energy and determination. It may signal emigration or just a move of house. Symbolically, it could mean a journey of the soul, or going to great lengths to achieve knowledge in this area. Whatever the journey, you must put your energy into it completely or it will fail to be the great adventure you had hoped it to be. There is help on the way to do this and a great surge of energy, so enjoy the ride, seek out new endeavors, and walk down the path with a bounce in your step. It is going to be great fun. You have confidence on your side, so let go and take the first step.

FIRST IMPRESSIONS

Queen of Wands

This woman is a friendly influence, obliging and helpful in every way. She wants to know how she can help you and will encourage you to follow your dream. This Queen is a decent, honest, and kind person, who could be in a position to help you earn a promotion with her guidance. She is the kind of friend you wish you had. Her laugh is contagious and she is just so much fun at parties. She is full of energy and a joy to know. Bubbly and vivacious, she always stands out for the others. I would say this woman is someone who lends an ear when you are down, or cheers you up when you need a boost. She is a good person, so look out for her in your circle of friends; she could be your new best friend.

FIRST IMPRESSIONS

King of Wands

This man is a charismatic leader; he could charm the birds out of the sky. He is powerful, energetic, and people are drawn to him. He does not have to command you to do as he wishes; people just do it because of his air of authority. He has a magnetic pull that draws admirers and lovers to him without him having to lift a finger. He likes to make an entrance and has enough flair and pizzazz to do that in style. This King is a natural-born artist who uses his skills in all areas to enhance any project he undertakes. He can be inspiring. Colleagues try to imitate him in some way because of his ability to stand out in the crowd and get the boss's eye, but they are in his shadow. He is a whirlwind of energy and a force to be reckoned with.

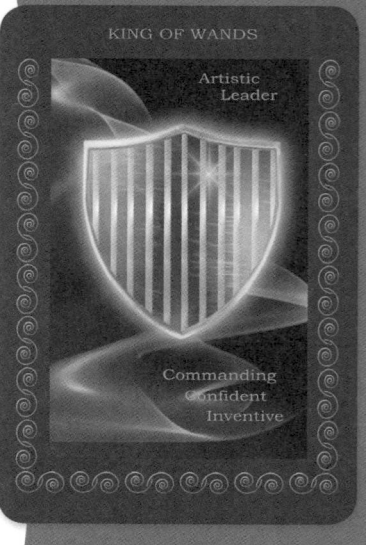

FIRST IMPRESSIONS

Ace of Cups

It is time to fall head over heels in love. This card tells you that love and more love is the answer. It heralds a time when you should open up your heart, let the love flow in, and then flow out again to those around you. Let the world know that you are looking for love and it will return that call. Let it shine out for all to see and trust in the fact that it will be returned in abundance. Feel your way through life now and let it bring you something wonderful. Aces are all about new things, so watch out for that new love. Actually, never mind watching out; you cannot miss this new love—it will knock you off your feet and send you off on cloud nine.

FIRST IMPRESSIONS

2 Cups

Love, marriage, companionship, union, a joint effort, or an affair is on the cards. It is a lovely feeling to have someone by your side, a wonderful companion who wants to share your life. Love is here to stay and you will find that people now offer support. A new lover enters the picture, or a colleague decides to help you. With this card in your spread, watch out for the one you will marry—he or she might be just around the corner. There is a healing of old wounds and letting past problems remain in the past. You are in a place where love is all around you and all you have to do is reach out and hold on tight.

FIRST IMPRESSIONS

3 Cups

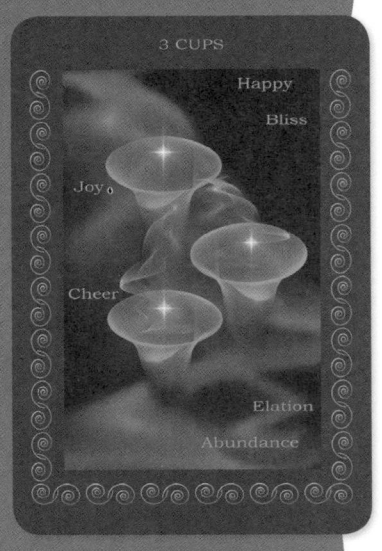

Happy conclusions, joy, a joining of forces, and sheer bliss are on the way. You could not pick a better card. People who love you want to celebrate with you. It is party time! You can enjoy this wholeheartedly and experience the bliss of having good friends, a gentle lover, and people around you who care. Celebration is at hand and those who love you will want to share this with you. Be prepared for many nights out in good company, and who knows, maybe you will find the ultimate in love, your soulmate, at one of these festivities. Experience the bliss and share the joy of knowing that the universe supports you.

FIRST IMPRESSIONS

4 Cups

An exciting offer is being handed to you, but you are so bored with your life and so discontent with your lot that you do not even see it. If you just reach out, you will find something more important in your life and something far more fulfilling. You are feeling sorry for yourself and this is preventing you from moving forward. An inspiring message or offer is on its way to you and it will uplift you. It will enhance your life and renew your zest for living. Seek this message: Reach out, grab it with both hands and make way for brighter days. Stop feeling sorry for yourself and see what you have in your grasp.

FIRST IMPRESSIONS

5 Cups

You can regret a loss with this card, but sometimes we are so caught up in the misery of that loss, we do not see the wonder we still have in our lives. Try to see it as a card of compensation, rather than loss—we are compensated by the fact that we still have some wonderful things and people in our lives who can comfort and console us. You may not see it now, but if you look for it, there will be a silver lining to chase away that big dark cloud over your head. Do not let despair blind you to the love you still have in your life.

FIRST IMPRESSIONS

6 Cups

Happy times are ahead of you. You are remembering the past, times when things were simple and joy was abundant. Remember these times and enjoy the fact that something from the past is returning into your life. It could be an old friend, or a family member you have not seen in ages, or it could just be that you are remembering how happy you were, when you trusted like a child and saw each day as a new opportunity to laugh and play. Find the child within you and ask it to come out to play again. Feel carefree and let your hair down; it is time to relax and let the world go by.

FIRST IMPRESSIONS

7 Cups

Here you are offered many things, but the choice you make is very important to how your life will turn out. You can choose the mystical pathway or the material path, but be careful you are making the **right** choice. Do not become so dreamy-eyed with the abundance of choices that you forget to think about the consequences. There are some lovely surprises coming, some lovely offers too, but choose only the ones that will bring you true happiness and not a fleeting moment of joy. Some of these offers will help you move forward in your spiritual work and some in your material; choose wisely. A little bit of both would be better in the end.

FIRST IMPRESSIONS

8 Cups

A card that heralds the letting go of old emotions, old relations, and old ideas. You are moving on, a little despondent, but there is hope in the not-too-distant future of a better, more fulfilling life. Keep moving forward; seek out your new adventures and fill your life with new things. You have become disheartened about your life and all the things you once held dear. The rule to follow is: If you do not like it, change it. It will make a difference if you do and bring with it a new enthusiasm for life.

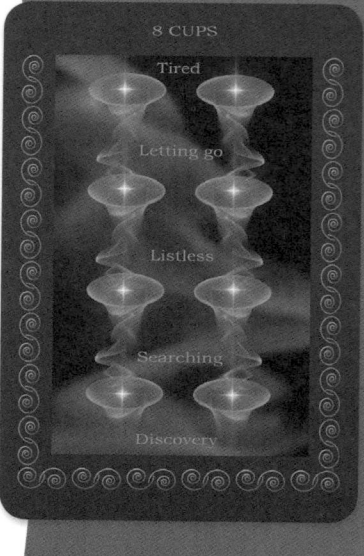

FIRST IMPRESSIONS

9 Cups

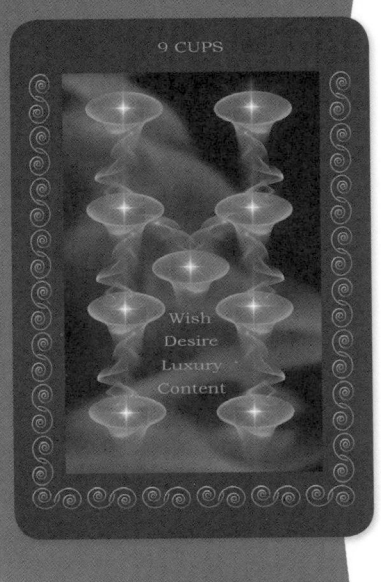

Wow! Your dreams come true, your wish is granted, and all your desires come to fruition. Need I say more? This is the card of fulfillment and contentment in achieving your goals. You can sit back and enjoy them, but remember to save a little of that thrilling feeling for the rainy days; you have so much of it now that you could sell it. Share this feeling with those close to you, as you are feeling so happy with yourself that your family will want to see you at your best and celebrate with you. Celebrations, parties and fun, fun, fun—that is the order of this card.

FIRST IMPRESSIONS

10 Cups

There is joy, happiness, and a complete feeling of contentment with this card. What more could you ask for? Nothing; you do not need anything else—you have it all with this card. It promises love, marriage, perfect balance in relationships, children, and the pot of gold at the end of the rainbow. Search for the bluebird of happiness and you will find it; it is there right over your head, just waiting for you to hear its song. Enjoy this time and remember to give thanks for the abundance in your life at present. It is a blessing to have such a feeling of contentment.

FIRST IMPRESSIONS

Page of Cups

This card calls to you to open up to all the wonderful things around you—like the flowers, the trees, and the people who love you. Page of Cups calls for you to receive messages of love, gifts of knowledge from unlikely sources, or just wonderful ideas that pop into your head. Let your heart rule your head and become like a child again. Throw open the doors and let the sunshine in. Play, be happy, enjoy the gift of life and let love in. This card calls for all this, and more, because something nice is coming and you need to open your heart to it. Let your emotions rule this day; trust in your destiny.

FIRST IMPRESSIONS

Knight of Cups

This person is a complete romantic. He will remember your birthday or anniversaries and will turn up at your door with gifts. He is a dreamer in every sense of the word. He sees only the beauty in the world and is sincere in his appraisal of those around him. An artist, he is full of dreams and desires to fill this world with beauty.

If this is an invitation to a party, it will be a wonderful occasion full of happy, loving people. He brings messages and inspiration to anyone who will listen and is aware of your needs and intuitive about your feelings. This Knight is a wonderful lover who will leave a flower on your pillow and make you a cup of coffee in the morning before he leaves.

FIRST IMPRESSIONS

Queen of Cups

Loving, dreamy, and intuitive: That is the Queen of Cups. She is devoted to whatever cause she is helping and will use her gifts of healing energy to give comfort to those around her. She exudes this energy; she will go out of her way to sort out your problems. She is a visionary, and knows just what to say in a difficult situation. She is a good friend, a wise woman, and someone you can trust. Look for this woman in the caring professions—a therapist who really listens or a psychiatrist who works hard to find the answers. She is devoted to helping others.

FIRST IMPRESSIONS

King of Cups

This is a very creative, kind, and tolerant sort of man. He is calm in his attitude, gentle in his approach, and his voice could bring healing to any crisis. He is a natural-born mediator, bringing his creative intelligence to every situation. He gives generously to charity and always lends an ear to those in need. He is a very good person to have on your side. His cup is ever flowing with kindness and humanitarianism. Not overly emotional, he can empathize with you and give good advice on how to deal with a problem. This man is a doctor or wonderfully creative teacher. He inspires people just through his actions.

FIRST IMPRESSIONS

Ace of Pentacles

Aces always show a new beginning, venture, or possibility for growth. So in this case, being Pentacles, it shows that there is an opportunity coming up to make big money, land that perfect job, or save a bit of money for a rainy day. It could herald a win of some sort that could help secure the future, or a job offer that brings in more money. Either way, this card is good for possible openings in your life to earn cash. Take it and trust that it will bring you security. Trust that the universe is offering you an opportunity to secure your finances and make headway for the coming years.

FIRST IMPRESSIONS

2 Pentacles

This is a lovely card; you are moving forward, embracing the idea of new challenges. You have balance in your life and are ready for something new. Financially you are okay, secure in the knowledge that you have paid attention to finances and your career. Now you are ready to take another step forward and you are enjoying the anticipation of what this could be. There is no hurry; you have time on your side. You are progressing smoothly, no bumps along the way and are having fun. This is a good card if you are seeking new adventures.

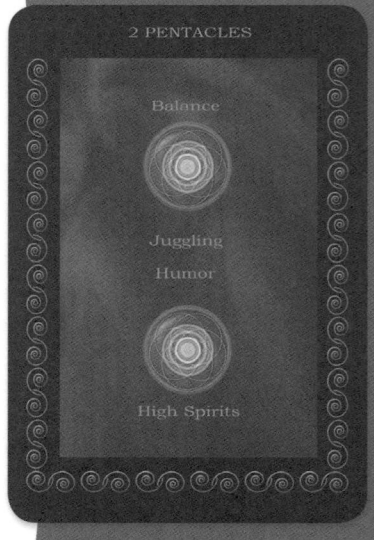

FIRST IMPRESSIONS

3 Pentacles

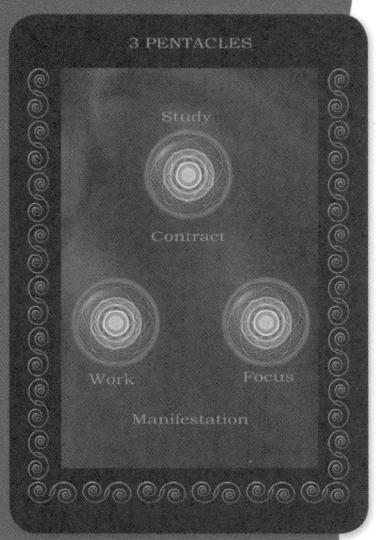

This card heralds teamwork, working with others, supporting them and being of service. Lack of ego and an ability to work alongside others is important here. Try to see the whole picture, let the ego go, and trust in your colleagues' ideas and input. This will help you go far. Timetables, schedules, and carefully, thought-out plans are important now. Try to get as many people to help you as possible; it will pay off in the end. Be inspired by others and enjoy the feeling of working together. Contribute to the group; allow their ideas and yours to combine into something that will benefit all concerned.

FIRST IMPRESSIONS

4 Pentacles

Control, miserly, blocked, closed, and *penny-pinching* are words that describe this card nicely—holding on with both hands to what you have gained and not wanting to share is a problem. It shows a fear of loss and poverty, even though there is enough to sustain you, **and** support others. Try not to hold on too tight or you will lose it all. This goes for money, relationships, and your children; let them enjoy their life, support them, trust them, and you will have more riches than you can count. Hold on too tight and you will lose out. Try to reach out and share your wealth, your feelings, and your life with others or you will have regrets.

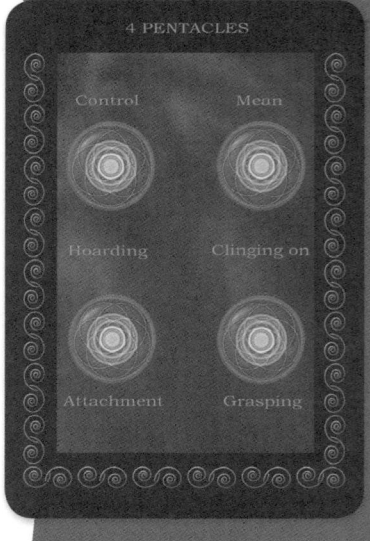

FIRST IMPRESSIONS

5 Pentacles

Picking this card shows that you are in need of something, and although there is help out there, you are so down in the dumps that you cannot see it. You feel left out in the cold, abandoned, and impoverished. But it does not have to be this way; there is help out there if you seek it.

Money is low and so is the feeling of there being anyone out there who cares. Here is the time to find the strength to get things going again; ask for that help and do not be too proud or too depressed to think that it is wrong to ask for it. You need help, so ask for it and trust it will come.

FIRST IMPRESSIONS

6 Pentacles

This card is all about gifts, sponsorship, support, and a helping hand. If you can give it, do so. If you need help, ask for it—it will be forthcoming. You can trust that the universe is going to help you in whatever way it can; you just have to ask and you will receive. It is a caring card and shows a situation where someone might need your help: An elderly person might need a lift to the store, or a child might need help with fixing their bicycle. It simply says for you to help someone and reap the rewards. You will feel much better for doing so. By letting others help you, you are helping someone else to feel good; so either way, it is a win-win situation. Try to be charitable when this card shows up. You are not alone; there is someone out there just waiting to help you.

FIRST IMPRESSIONS

7 Pentacles

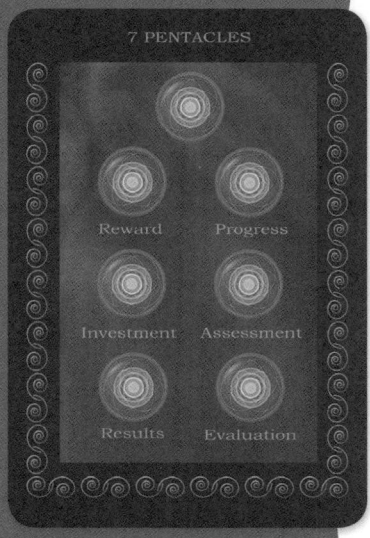

You have worked hard, tallied up the books, and now you are assessing your status in life. You have accumulated much, but want to be sure that it is enough. It is; you have used common sense in your approach and saved for a rainy day. You will succeed, because you are not pushing forward without thinking of where you have been and how much you have gained. You are methodical in your approach and this will stand you in good stead.

Enjoy your rewards, reap the benefits and carry on. There is nothing stopping you. Just make sure you learn to enjoy the benefits and not work too hard trying to accumulate more, or you will lose out, despite your wealth.

FIRST IMPRESSIONS

8 Pentacles

If you want to succeed, you have to put the work in. Pay attention to detail, maybe even work longer hours, but the key here is to **enjoy** the work. Find pleasure in producing the finished product, knowing that you did your best and are proud of your piece.

Learning new skills to help you achieve greater things and becoming absorbed in your efforts will show you the way to success in everything you do. If you put the work in you can achieve anything you desire. Diligence and hard work show great results.

FIRST IMPRESSIONS

9 Pentacles

Being self-reliant is important; trust in your abilities. Making it on your own is what this card represents. Believe that your way is the best way forward because it is; you have come to this conclusion through diligence and hard work, so have faith in *you*.

Enjoy the finer things in life and use tact and diplomacy in all your dealings with people. This card speaks of refinement, luxury, and gracious pursuits. Be happy with your life and your achievements; enjoy the independence they bring. Self-reliance, restraint, and discipline in your pursuits make you into a very self-sufficient person.

FIRST IMPRESSIONS

10 Pentacles

This is a wonderful card; it shows you've made it and can relax in the secure knowledge that this is a permanent position. This card conjures up the wealthy retired person who has worked hard, saved up hard-earned cash, and is now reaping the benefits. It tells you that if you stick with it, you can become self-assured in your surroundings and build a happy and secure life. Trust in the tried and tested with this card. If it works, stick with it, and enjoy the rewards. See your ventures flourish and enjoy the ride because this card tells you that the success is here to stay. You have no money worries and you feel confident.

FIRST IMPRESSIONS

Page of Pentacles

Pages, to me, speak of something you are discovering and therefore need to learn more about. In the case of Pentacles, it would have something to do with being practical and sensible. For example, if you want a job as a brain surgeon, then it would be wise to study and not jump in with two feet saying you read a book on Indian Head Massage. This card heralds caution, diligence, and common sense in your approach to something you want to achieve. It tells of a time when you should seek your fortune, believe in yourself and your abilities, and trust that the universe is showing you the way.

FIRST IMPRESSIONS